About
Skill Builders
Español en Casa
Spanish at Home
by Ellen Parrish

Welcome to RBP Books' Skill Builders™ series. Like our Summer Bridge Activities collection, the Skill Builders™ series is designed to make learning both fun and rewarding.

Skill Builders™ Spanish—*Español en Casa* helps beginning Spanish students increase their vocabulary as they explore the Valenzuelas' home and learn Spanish words for objects they may see in their own home every day. This level 2 Spanish book also includes simple Spanish sentences, and an Advanced Concepts section introduces basic verb conjugations and a fun approach to grammatical gender. Activities are fun and designed to give plenty of practice and review to help reinforce new vocabulary at an easy pace. This makes language acquisition *muy fácil* (really easy).

Learning is more effective when approached with an element of fun and enthusiasm—just as most children approach life. That's why the Skill Builders™ combine entertaining and academically sound exercises with eye-catching graphics and fun themes—to make reviewing basic skills at school or home fun and effective, for both you and your budding scholars.

Table of Contents

La casa Valenzuela—The Valenzuela Home

¡Bienvenidos!

(Welcome!)

¡Adelante!

(Come in!)

Bienvenidos means "welcome." *Adelante* means "Come on in." When you practice writing words out, it helps you learn them. Try it.

Pronunciation Key

Las vocales—The Vowels   <u>As used in the English word:</u>

A—(ah)   what
E—(eh)   men
I—(ee)   machine
O—(oh)   open
U—(oo)   June

Otras letras especiales—Other Special Letters

ñ—(en-yeh)   <u>Example</u>: mañana—mah-nyah-nah
ll—(eh-yeh)   <u>Example</u>: amarillo—ah-mah-ree-yoh
ch—(che)   <u>Example</u>: chico—chee-coh
rr—(eh-rre: a long trill or rolled *r*)   <u>Example</u>: burro—boo-r-r-r-o

La familia Valenzuela—The Valenzuela Family

Practice writing the Spanish words on the lines.

el papá
father

la mamá
mother

el hermano
brother

la hermana
sister

el bebé
the baby

el perro
dog

el gato
cat

¿Quién es?—Who is it?

Write each answer using the Word Bank below.

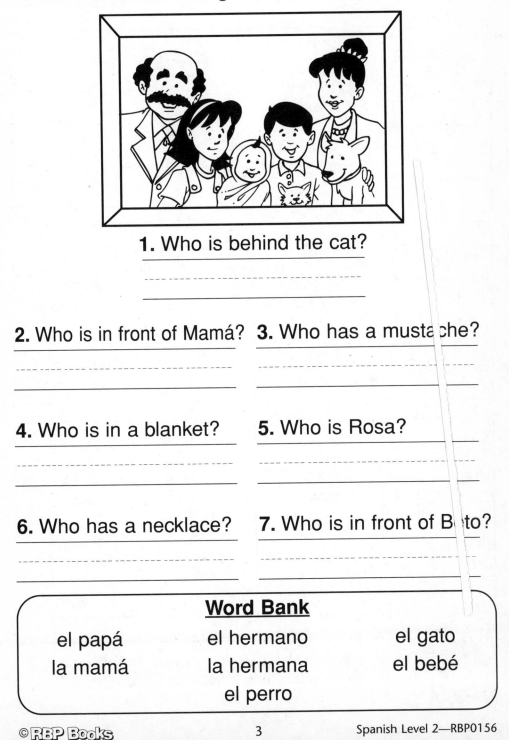

1. Who is behind the cat?

----

2. Who is in front of Mamá?

----

3. Who has a mustache?

----

4. Who is in a blanket?

----

5. Who is Rosa?

----

6. Who has a necklace?

----

7. Who is in front of Beto?

Word Bank

el papá	el hermano	el gato
la mamá	la hermana	el bebé
	el perro	

En la cocina—In the Kitchen

Practice writing the Spanish words on the lines.

horno
oven

vaso
glass

refrigerador
refrigerator

plato
plate

mesa
table

silla
chair

Try out some of these words on your friends and family. You are building a Spanish vocabulary.

En la cocina—In the Kitchen

Practice writing the Spanish words on the lines.

lavaplatos
dishwasher

cuchillo
knife

tenedor
fork

espátula
spatula

olla
pot

cuchara
spoon

¡Bien!
(Good!)

Lo que se hace en la cocina—
What We Do in the Kitchen

Practice writing the Spanish words on the lines.

cocinar
to cook

cortar
to cut

mezclar
to mix

comer
to eat

lavar los
platos
to wash the
dishes

barrer
to sweep

Do you help out in the kitchen at home?
Sometimes I wash the dishes. *(A veces lavo los platos.)*

Palabras nuevas para mezclar salsa—Salsa Vocabulary

Use these new vocabulary words to follow the recipe on the next page.

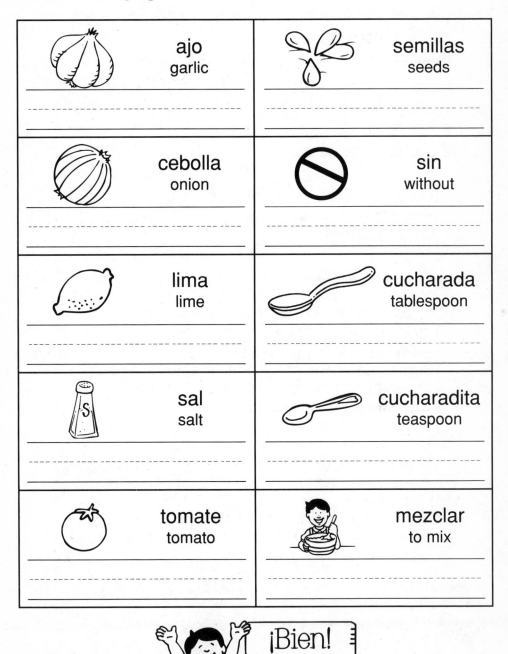

ajo garlic		**semillas** seeds	
cebolla onion		**sin** without	
lima lime		**cucharada** tablespoon	
sal salt		**cucharadita** teaspoon	
tomate tomato		**mezclar** to mix	

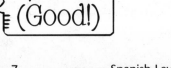

¡Bien! (Good!)

7

Salsa fresca—Fresh Salsa

3 tomates medianos, sin semillas, cortados
1 cebolla mediana, cortada
3 dientes del ajo, cortados muy pequeños
1 jalapeño mediano, sin semillas, cortado muy pequeño
2 cucharadas de cilantro fresco, cortado muy pequeño
2 cucharadas de jugo de lima
1/2 cucharadita de sal

Mezcla todo, ponlo en un bol cubierto, ponlo en el refrigerador por al menos una hora. Sírvelo con tortillas del maiz fritas.

3 medium tomatoes, seeded and chopped
1 medium onion, chopped
3 cloves garlic, finely chopped
1 medium jalapeño seeded and finely chopped
2 tablespoons fresh cilantro, finely chopped
2 tablespoons lime juice
1/2 teaspoon salt

Mix all ingredients together in a bowl, cover and refrigerate at least 1 hour to blend flavors. Serve with tortilla chips.

¡Disfruta! (Enjoy!)

Salsa fresca—Fresh Salsa

Color the picture of the Valenzuela family eating
chips and *salsa fresca*.

Apareemos—Matching

Draw a line from the item in the salsa recipe to its Spanish word.

tomate

semillas

cebolla

ajo

jalapeño

cucharada

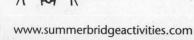

¡Es tiempo de limpiar! (It's time to clean up!)

Apareemos—Matching

Draw a line from the item in the salsa recipe to its Spanish word.

tortillas de maiz fritas

cucharadita

sal

bol

refrigerador

lima

¡Busca! Cosas de la cocina—Kitchen Word Search

Find and circle the Spanish vocabulary words for common kitchen items and actions.

```
r  n  z  r  e  r  r  a  b  e  c  w  r  l
e  s  p  a  t  u  l  a  t  y  n  e  a  w
o  t  a  l  p  a  r  r  m  d  f  v  s  r
c  r  v  h  l  a  e  e  c  r  a  e  a  a
r  n  x  l  l  m  s  c  i  p  r  t  c  k
c  p  i  c  o  a  o  g  l  o  r  u  o  s
j  s  z  c  t  l  e  a  d  o  c  l  s  r
a  e  k  t  l  r  t  e  c  h  d  g  a  f
m  r  z  a  a  o  n  y  i  m  y  n  v  l
h  w  a  d  s  e  u  l  y  s  i  n  i  s
z  o  o  h  t  x  l  h  l  c  e  y  m  p
j  r  h  x  b  o  r  h  o  r  n  o  d  e
m  n  e  j  y  u  u  c  y  d  n  e  v  l
z  s  e  w  b  n  b  j  j  x  c  w  m  p
```

Word Bank

horno	tenedor	comer	silla
refrigerador	vaso	espátula	cocinar
lavaplatos	plato	olla	cortar
barrer	cuchillo	mesa	mezclar

¿Te gusta buscar palabras? ¡A mí sí! (Do you like word searches? I do!)

El dormitorio—The Bedroom

Practice writing out the vocabulary words. Color the picture of Rosa's room.

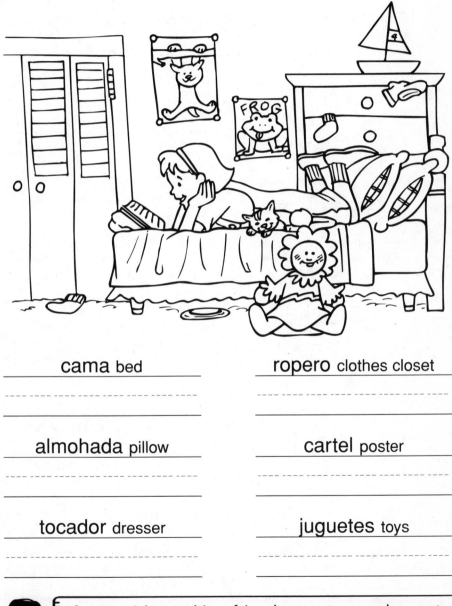

cama bed

ropero clothes closet

almohada pillow

cartel poster

tocador dresser

juguetes toys

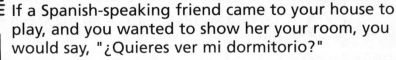

If a Spanish-speaking friend came to your house to play, and you wanted to show her your room, you would say, "¿Quieres ver mi dormitorio?"

La Ropa—Clothing

Practice writing out the vocabulary words.

"¡Limpia el dormitorio ahora mismo!"

zapatos

shoes

_____

- - - - - - - - - - - - - - - - - - -

_____

camiseta

T-shirt

_____

- - - - - - - - - - - - - - - - - - -

_____

chaqueta

jacket

_____

- - - - - - - - - - - - - - - - - - -

_____

falda

skirt

_____

- - - - - - - - - - - - - - - - - - -

_____

pantalones

pants

_____

- - - - - - - - - - - - - - - - - - -

_____

gorra

cap

_____

- - - - - - - - - - - - - - - - - - -

_____

My dad wants me to clean my room right now.

El laberinto—The Maze

Help Rosa find the dirty clothes hamper.

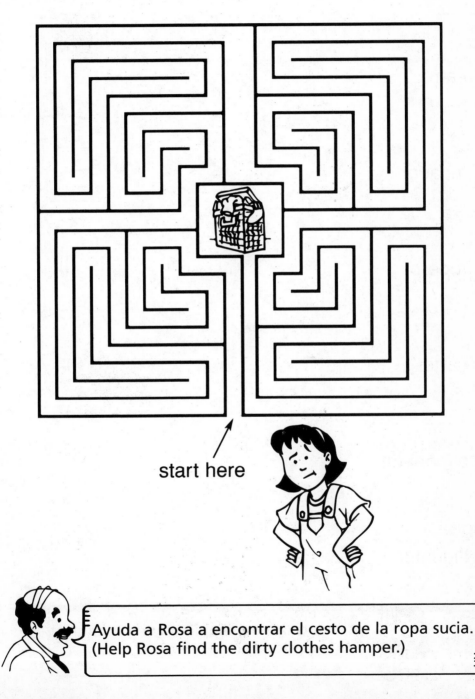

start here

Ayuda a Rosa a encontrar el cesto de la ropa sucia.
(Help Rosa find the dirty clothes hamper.)

Apareemos—Matching

Draw a line from the vocabulary word to its corresponding picture.

cama

tocador

ropero

cartel

almohada

juguete

 ¡Ahora todo está limpio en el dormitorio!
(My room is all clean now!)

Apareemos—Matching

Draw a line from the vocabulary word to its corresponding picture.

gorra

falda

chaqueta

falda

zapatos

pantalones

¡Bien!
(Good!)

En el sótano—In the Basement

Practice writing the Spanish words on the lines.

secadora dryer

pinza clothespin

lavadora washer

gancho hanger

jabón en polvo laundry soap

ropa clothes

Aquí lavamos la ropa.
(This is where we do our laundry.)

Frases útiles—Useful Phrases

Practice writing the Spanish phrases.

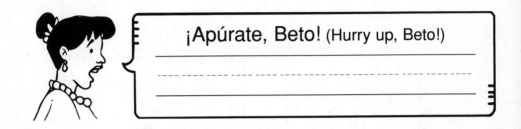

¡Apúrate, Beto! (Hurry up, Beto!)

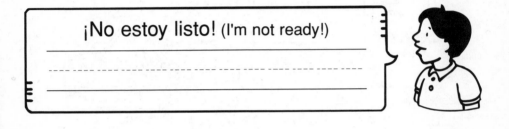

¡No estoy listo! (I'm not ready!)

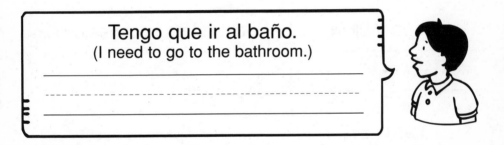

Tengo que ir al baño.
(I need to go to the bathroom.)

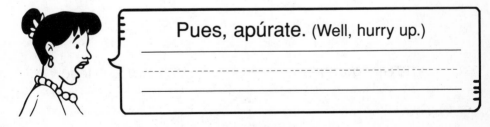

Pues, apúrate. (Well, hurry up.)

Salgamos—Let's Go Outside

Practice writing out the vocabulary words.

buzón mailbox

_____

- - - - - - - - - - - - -

_____

entrada de coches driveway

_____

- - - - - - - - - - - - -

_____

carro car

_____

- - - - - - - - - - - - -

_____

puerta door

_____

- - - - - - - - - - - - -

_____

garaje garage

_____

- - - - - - - - - - - - -

_____

ventana window

_____

- - - - - - - - - - - - -

_____

Ven gatito. (Here kitty.) I'm looking for my kitty.

Salgamos—Let's Go Outside

Practice writing out the vocabulary words.

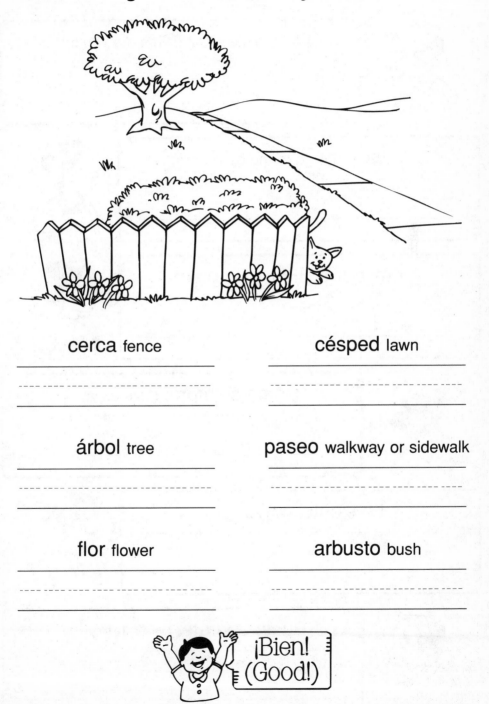

cerca fence

césped lawn

árbol tree

paseo walkway or sidewalk

flor flower

arbusto bush

¡Bien!
(Good!)

No te olvides—Don't Forget

Practice writing the Spanish phrases.

¿Qué olvidaste? (What did you forget?)

Ir al baño (to go to the bathroom)

Y mi gorra (and my ball cap)

Como siempre. (Like always.)

Lo siento. (I'm sorry.)

Pues, apúrate. (Well, hurry up.)

Rompecabeza—Crossword Puzzle

Complete the puzzle using the Spanish words for things outside.

Across
3. tree
4. car
7. door

Down
1. sidewalk
2. flower
4. lawn
5. window
6. garage

¿Sabías? (Did you know?) The Spanish word for *puzzle* means "*head breaker!*"

El baño—The Bathroom

Practice writing out the vocabulary words.

lavamanos sink
_____
- -
_____

cepillo para el pelo hairbrush
_____
- -
_____

jabón soap
_____
- -
_____

espejo mirror
_____
- -
_____

loción lotion
_____
- -
_____

peine comb
_____
- -
_____

¡Ah, mi gorra está debajo del lavamanos!
(Aha! My ball cap is under the sink!)

El baño—The Bathroom

Practice writing out the vocabulary words.

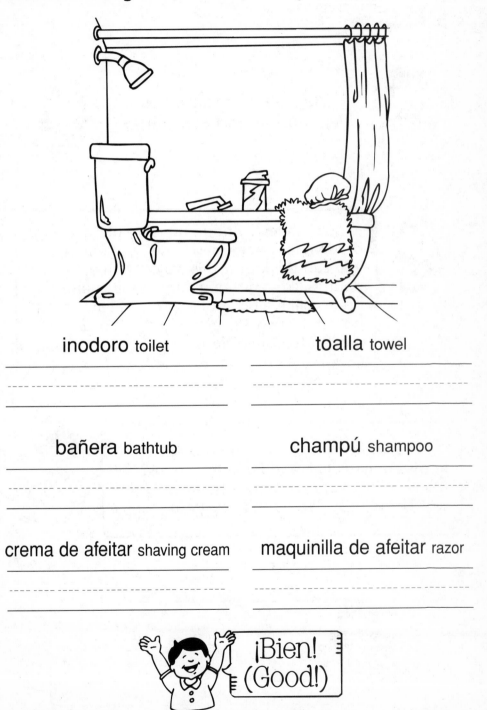

inodoro toilet

toalla towel

bañera bathtub

champú shampoo

crema de afeitar shaving cream

maquinilla de afeitar razor

¡Bien!
(Good!)

Algo sobre los nombres—
Something about Nouns

Masculino y feminino
(Masculine and Feminine)

In Spanish, every noun (person, place, thing, or idea) is either "masculine" or "feminine". You can think of it this way: a feminine noun is like a girl noun and a masculine noun is like a boy noun. It may seem funny, but that's how we do it. And it is usually easy to tell the difference.

Do you know how to tell the difference between masculine and feminine nouns? Many "boy" words end in *o* and many girl words end in *a*. Like our names: Bet**o**

and Ros**a**

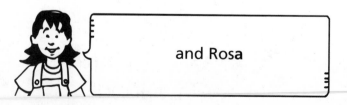

Nombres femininos—
Feminine Nouns

Draw a circle around all of the "girl" nouns below.

perro	carro	cebolla	puerta
gato	comida	niño	ventana
ajo	cocina	espejo	arbusto
pelota	gorra	baño	familia

I remember the "girl" nouns by thinking that a small *a* has a tail like a girl's ponytail.

And the "boy" noun ending, *o*, is like an open mouth!

Apareemos—Matching

Draw a line from the Spanish word to the correct picture.

inodoro

cepillo para el pelo

lavamanos

peine

toalla

maquinilla de afeitar

Yo lo hago esto cada mañana.
(I do this every morning.)

Apareemos—Matching

Draw a line from the Spanish word to the correct picture.

crema de afeitar

jabón

loción

bañera

espejo

champú

¡Bien!
(Good!)

Muy divertido—Lots of Fun

Color Beto and the dog playing.

El carro—The Car

Practice writing the Spanish words on the lines.

llanta
tire

----

farol
headlight

----

volante
steering wheel

----

parachoques
bumper

----

cinturón de seguridad
seatbelt

----

conductor
driver

¡Vámonos! ¿Quién quiere ir por un helado?
(Come on! Who wants to go for ice cream?)

Spanish Level 2—RBP0156

En el traspatio—In the Backyard

Practice writing the Spanish word on the lines.

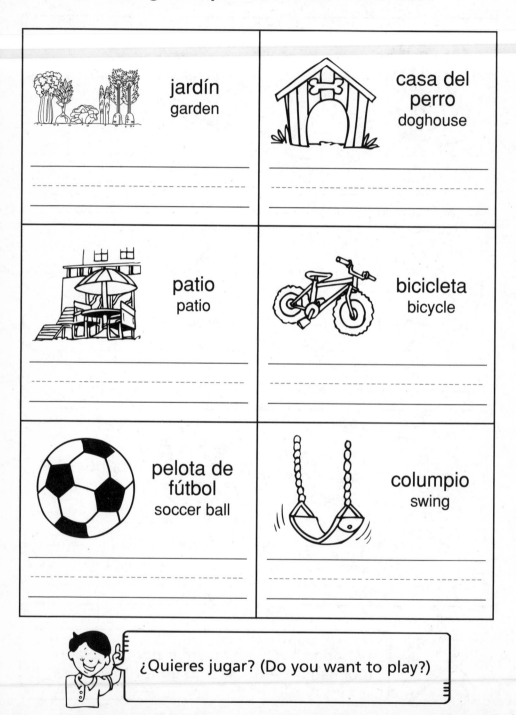

jardín
garden

_____
- - - - - - - - - - - - - - - - - - -
_____

casa del perro
doghouse

_____
- - - - - - - - - - - - - - - - - - -
_____

patio
patio

_____
- - - - - - - - - - - - - - - - - - -
_____

bicicleta
bicycle

_____
- - - - - - - - - - - - - - - - - - -
_____

pelota de fútbol
soccer ball

_____
- - - - - - - - - - - - - - - - - - -
_____

columpio
swing

_____
- - - - - - - - - - - - - - - - - - -
_____

¿Quieres jugar? (Do you want to play?)

Rompecabeza—Crossword Puzzle

Complete the puzzle using the Spanish words for parts of a car.

Across
3. driver
4. headlight
5. steering wheel
6. seatbelt

Down
1. tire
2. bumper

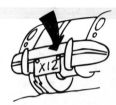

Spanish Level 2—RBP0156

La hora de dormir—Time for Bed

¿Ya te cepillaste los dientes, mija?
(Have you brushed your teeth, honey?)

Sí. (Yes.)
Pero tengo sed. (But I'm thirsty.)

Hay un vaso de agua cerca de tu almohada.
(There's a glass of water right next to your pillow.)

Ah, gracias. (Oh, thanks.)

La hora de dormir—Time for Bed

Dulces sueños. (Sweet dreams.)

¿Mamá, me traes el libro?
(Mom, will you bring me my book?)

Claro que sí, pero lee sólo por cinco minutos.
(Sure, but you can read for only five minutes.)

Te prometo.
(I promise.)

Acciónes—Actions

oler
to smell

gritar
to shout

jugar
to play

correr
to run

Acciónes—Actions

brincar
to jump

caer
to fall

llorar
to cry

descansar
to rest

Nombres masculinos—
Masculine Nouns

Draw a circle around all of the "boy" nouns below.

dormitorio	agua	pelota	libro
llanta	bicicleta	vaso	patio
sueño	cepillo	lavabo	zapato
cinco	crema	casa	camisa

Hay muchas palabras masculinas.
(There are lots of masculine words.)

Rompecabeza—Crossword Puzzle

Complete the puzzle using the Spanish words for things in the backyard.

Across
2. soccer ball
3. doghouse
5. bicycle

Down
1. garden
3. swing
4. patio

¡Cuidado con la pelota y mi jardín! (Careful with that ball and my garden!)

Spanish Level 2—RBP0156

Apareemos—Matching

Match the correct action word with its picture.

Smelling a flower,
_____

then jumping,
_____

then yelling,
_____

then crying.
_____

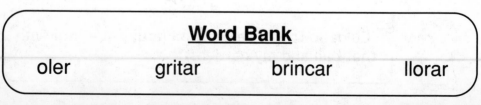

Word Bank

| oler | gritar | brincar | llorar |

En la sala—In the Living Room

Practice writing the vocabulary words.

sofá sofa	**alfombra** rug
pintura painting	**televisión** television
estéreo stereo	**lámpara** lamp
cortina curtain	**cojín** cushion

¡Qué lindas son las flores!
(How pretty the flowers are!)

El niño de los vecinos—The Neighbor Boy

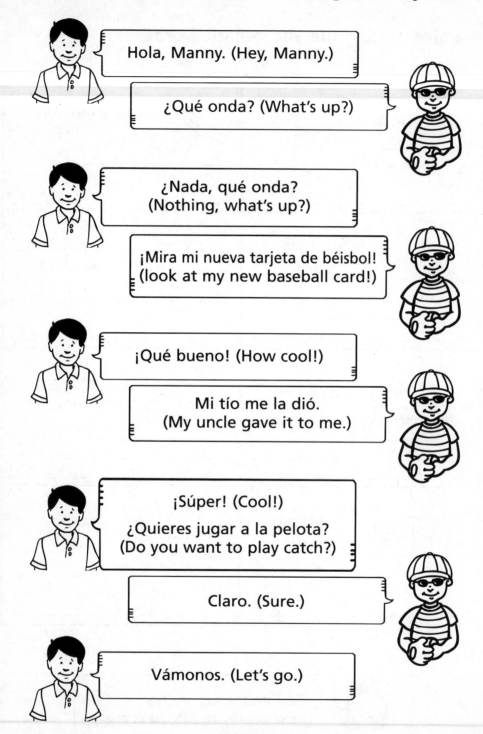

Hola, Manny. (Hey, Manny.)

¿Qué onda? (What's up?)

¿Nada, qué onda?
(Nothing, what's up?)

¡Mira mi nueva tarjeta de béisbol!
(look at my new baseball card!)

¡Qué bueno! (How cool!)

Mi tío me la dió.
(My uncle gave it to me.)

¡Súper! (Cool!)
¿Quieres jugar a la pelota?
(Do you want to play catch?)

Claro. (Sure.)

Vámonos. (Let's go.)

Las herramientas—Tools

Practice writing out the vocabulary words.

martillo
hammer

alicates
pliers

destornillador
screwdriver

clavo
nail

cinta métrica
tape measure

30'

taladro
drill

tornillos
screws

sierra
saw

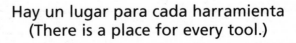

Hay un lugar para cada harramienta
(There is a place for every tool.)

¡Busca! Los muebles—Furniture Word Search

Find and circle the Spanish vocabulary words.

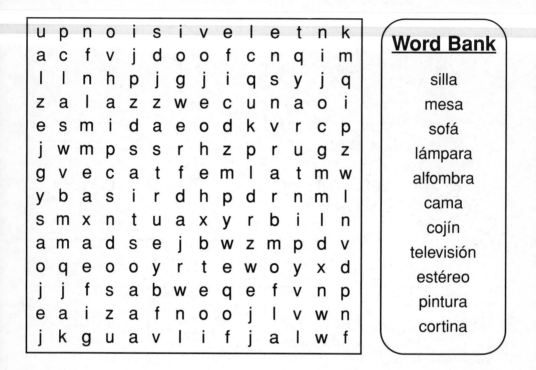

```
u p n o i s i v e l e t n k
a c f v j d o o f c n q i m
l l n h p j g j i q s y j q
z a l a z z w e c u n a o i
e s m i d a e o d k v r c p
j w m p s s r h z p r u g z
g v e c a t f e m l a t m w
y b a s i r d h p d r n m l
s m x n t u a x y r b i l n
a m a d s e j b w z m p d v
o q e o o y r t e w o y x d
j j f s a b w e q e f v n p
e a i z a f n o o j l v w n
j k g u a v l i f j a l w f
```

Word Bank

silla

mesa

sofá

lámpara

alfombra

cama

cojín

televisión

estéreo

pintura

cortina

Apareemos—Matching

Draw a line from the Spanish word to the correct picture.

silla

mesa

sofá

lámpara

alfombra

cama

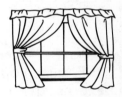

cojín

televisión

estéreo

pintura

cortina

¡Ya sabes tantas palabras en español!
(You already know so many Spanish words!)

Reglas de los verbos—
Rules for Verbs

Spanish verbs are expressed differently than English verbs. Each verb "agrees" with the person, place, thing, or idea that it is working with. To show this, the ending of the main verb changes. Here's how it works:

Hablar (to talk)	
hablo (I talk)	hablamos (we talk)
hablas (you talk)	
habla (he, she, or it talks)	hablan (they talk)

In English you would use two words to express the idea "I talk." In Spanish, the way you use the verb tells you who or what is talking.

"I speak Spanish" means the same thing as "Hablo español."

These rules are different than the rules for English, but as you learn to use them, you will see that they work really well. The end result is successful communication.

¡Bien!
(Good!)

Los verbos con *ar*—*ar* Verbs

Verbs end in either *-ar*, *-er*, or *-ir* in Spanish. All of the verbs below are *-ar* verbs. They follow the rules described on page 46.

described on page 46.

Write out the verbs' different endings below as shown in the example.

Brincar (to jump)			
(I)	brinco	brincamos	*(we)*
(you)	brincas		
(he, she, or it)	brinca	brincan	*(they)*

Hablar (to talk)			
(I)			*(we)*
(you)			
(he, she, or it)			*(they)*

Cantar (to sing)			
(I)			*(we)*
(you)			
(he, she, or it)			*(they)*

Limpiar (to clean)			
(I)			*(we)*
(you)			
(he, she, or it)			*(they)*

Cortar (to cut)			
(I)			*(we)*
(you)			
(he, she, or it)			*(they)*

Descansar (to rest)			
(I)			*(we)*
(you)			
(he, she, or it)			*(they)*

Rompecabeza—Crossword Puzzle

Complete the puzzle using the Spanish words for tools.

Across
1. hammer
4. nail
7. screwdriver

Down
2. pliers
3. tape measure
5. saw
6. screws
8. drill

¿Quién tiene el martillo ahora?
(Who has my hammer now?)

Los verbos con *er*—*er* Verbs

Let's keep working on verbs. All of the verbs below end in -*er*. They follow the same rules as the -*ar* verbs, but they end differently.

Write out the verbs' different endings below as shown in the example.

Comer (to eat)			
(I)	como	comemos	*(we)*
(you)	comes		
(he, she, or it)	come	comen	*(they)*

Barrer (to sweep)			
(I)			*(we)*
(you)			
(he, she, or it)			*(they)*

Correr (to run)			
(I)			*(we)*
(you)			
(he, she, or it)			*(they)*

Beber (to drink)			
(I)			*(we)*
(you)			
(he, she, or it)			*(they)*

Depender (to depend)			
(I)			*(we)*
(you)			
(he, she, or it)			*(they)*

Leer (to read)			
(I)			*(we)*
(you)			
(he, she, or it)			*(they)*

Los verbos con *ir*—*ir* Verbs

Write out the verbs' different endings below as shown in the example:

Let's look at the *-ir* verbs. These *-ir* verbs take the same endings and follow the same rules as the *-er* verbs, except the "we" version. That ending is *-imos*, as in *decidimos*.

Decidir (to decide)

(I)	decido	decidimos	(we)
(you)	decides		
(he, she, or it)	decide	deciden	(they)

Vivir (to live)

(I)			(we)
(you)			
(he, she, or it)			(they)

Subir (to go up)

(I)			(we)
(you)			
(he, she, or it)			(they)

Escribir (to write)

(I)			(we)
(you)			
(he, she, or it)			(they)

Unir (to unite)

(I)			(we)
(you)			
(he, she, or it)			(they)

Cubrir (to cover)

(I)			(we)
(you)			
(he, she, or it)			(they)

En el cuarto del bebé—In the Nursery

Practice writing the Spanish words on the lines.

cuna
crib

_____

chupete
pacifier

_____

pañal
diaper

_____

bloques
blocks

_____

cochecito de niño
stroller

_____

manta
blanket

_____

muñeco de peluche
stuffed toy

_____

móvil
mobile

_____

¡Qué precioso cuando está durmiendo!
(How precious when he's sleeping!)

¿Qué palabra es la correcta?—Which word is correct?

Follow the example and circle the correct form of each verb in the following sentences. Refer to the verb tables to make sure you choose the right verb.

1. Beto y Manny (hablo (hablan) hablamos) de sus tarjetas de béisbol favoritas.
   (Beto and Manny talk about their favorite baseball cards.)

2. El bebé (lloras llora lloran) si no tiene su chupete.
   (The baby cries if he doesn't have his pacifier.)

3. (Comes Comen Comemos) cada noche a las seis.
   (We eat every night at six o'clock on the dot.)

4. Ellos (corren corremos corre) de una casa a otra cuando están jugando.
   (They run from one house to the other when they are playing.)

5. Rosa (limpia, limpio, limpiamos) su dormitorio
   (Rosa cleans her room)

6. El anciano de nuestra calle (vivimos vivo vive) solo.
   (The old man on our street lives alone.)

¡Bien! (Good!)

¿Qué palabra es la correcta?—Which word is correct?

Circle the correct form of each verb in the following sentences. Refer to the verb tables to make sure you choose the right verb.

7. Mi mamá y mi papá (beben bebemos bebes) una taza de café cada mañana.
(My mom and dad drink a cup of coffee every morning.)

8. ¿Cómo (subimos subo sube) el gato al árbol?
(How does the cat go up the tree?)

9. Mamá le (cantan canta cantamos) una canción al bebé.
(Mom sings a song to the baby.)

10. Mi hermano y yo (leemos leen leo) por media hora cada día.
(My brother and I read for half an hour every day.)

11. Yo (Barro Barren Barres) el piso de la cocina.
(I sweep the kitchen floor.)

12. Papá le (corta cortamos corto) el pelo a Beto cada dos meses.
(Dad cuts Beto's hair every two months.)

¡Bien!
(Good!)

Los animales domésticos—Pets

Write the Spanish words on the lines.

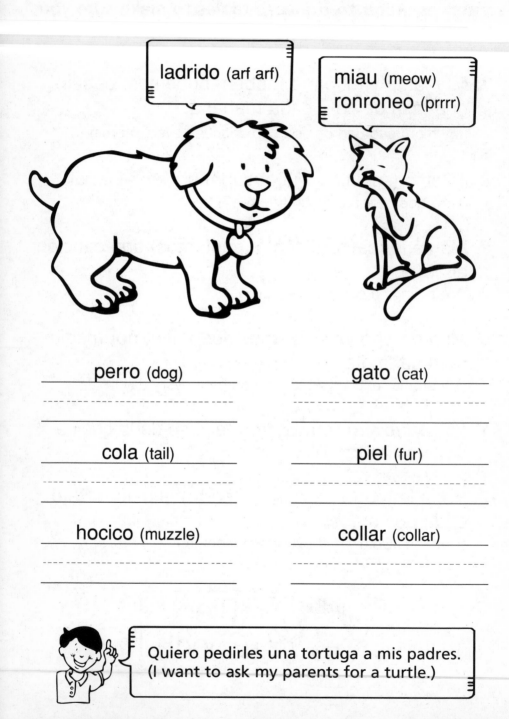

ladrido (arf arf)

miau (meow)
ronroneo (prrrr)

perro (dog)

gato (cat)

cola (tail)

piel (fur)

hocico (muzzle)

collar (collar)

Quiero pedirles una tortuga a mis padres.
(I want to ask my parents for a turtle.)

Rompecabeza—Nursery Crossword Puzzle

Complete the puzzle using the Spanish words for things you would find in a nursery.

Across
2. stuffed toy
5. blocks
6. diaper
7. blanket

Down
1. stroller
3. pacifier
4. crib
7. mobile

¡Ah, el martillo! (Oh, there's my hammer!)

Nosotros jugamos con el bebé—We Play with the Baby

Trátalo. (Try it.)

Papas y Papás

Papas y papas para papá,
papas y papas para mamá.
Las quemaditas para papá,
las calientitas para mamá.

Papas y papas para papá,
papas y papas para mamá.
Las quemaditas para papá,
las calientitas para mamá.

Potatoes for daddy,
potatoes for mommy.
The brown ones for daddy,
the hot ones for mommy.

Potatoes for daddy,
potatoes for mommy.
The brown ones for daddy,
the hot ones for mommy.

This is a clapping game like patty cake that you can play with babies and toddlers.

 ¿Puedo jugar también? (Can I play too?)

Nosotros jugamos con el bebé—We Play with the Baby

Ahora es mi turno. (Now it's my turn.)

Play with the baby's hand when you sing this.

Que linda manita

Que linda manita
Que tiene el bebé
Que linda, que mona,
Que bonita es.
Pequeños deditos,
Rayitos de sol
Que gire, que gire
Como un girasol.

Move your hand in a circle while you sing so the baby can copy you.

How pretty, how small,
Is this baby's sweet hand.
Lovely, oh lovely!
How pretty is his hand.
Tiny little fingers
Like a ray of sun,
Spinning and turning
Like a bright sunflower.

Spanish Level 2—RBP0156

Apareemos—Matching

Draw a line from the Spanish word to the correct picture.

gato

hocico

cola

piel

collar

perro

¡Bien!
(Good!)

En el estudio—In the Study

Practice writing out the vocabulary words.

cubo de la basura
trash can

_____

impresora
printer

_____

estantería
shelves
_____

computadora
computer
_____

teléfono
telephone
_____

resma de papel
ream of paper

_____

grapadora
stapler

_____

escritorio
desk

_____

fax
fax

_____

Trabajo aquí en casa. Es muy conveniente.
(I work here at home. It's very convenient.)

¡Busca! El estudio—
Study Word Search

```
w r x j c o i r o t i r c s e
g t t r l k k r s d e l j t e
x h x m q h e o b i b g l n s
a c i n u t b b j e a o k i s
f c o m p u t a d o r a g f q
e o k y u t i m p r e s o r a
j z p i s g r a p a d o r a d
t a r u s a b a l e d o b u c
e h v n n v g r j i t w t j k
l b h q e a i r e t n a t s e
e y l e p a p e d a m s e r r
f v g t m q s d i l s n i w p
o j c x a x n b p y c z c d a
n z h v d a l o n p j x c y k
o q c g a l b y i z n l s x v
```

Word Bank

cubo de la basura

impresora

estantería

computadora

teléfono

resma de papel

grapadora

escritorio

fax

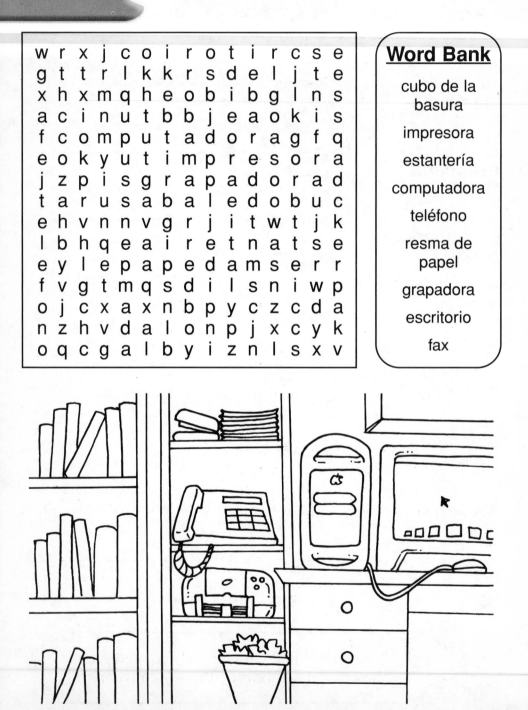

Artículos definidos e indefinidos—
Definite and Indefinite Articles

You can see the difference between *definite* and *indefinite* articles in the following sentences. But for now, don't worry about why we call these "artículos".

We use them all the time in English and Spanish. They work with nouns to give us more information about the noun.

Look at the difference:

Pick <u>a</u> flower.
Pick <u>the</u> red flower.

The difference between the *definite* and *indefinite* article has to do with whether we are talking about a specific flower or any flower at all.

<u>The</u> red flower is a specific, or *definite* flower.

Artículos definidos plurales—
Plural Articles

In English, the definite article is the word <u>the</u> whether the noun it introduces is singular or plural.

We say:
    <u>The</u> plate
    <u>The</u> plates

Whether it's one plate or a whole stack, when you have certain plates in mind you'll use <u>the</u>.

In Spanish the definite article changes, depending on whether the noun is singular or plural.

Decimos:
    <u>El</u> plato
    <u>Los</u> platos

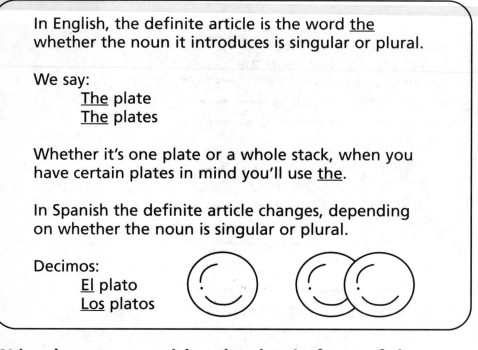

Write the correct article, *el* or *los,* in front of the nouns below.

Juego con _____ perro.
(I play with the dog.)

Mamá lava _____ platos.
(Mom washes the plates.)

Esperamos en _____ carro.
(We wait in the car.)

_____ zapatos están muy sucios.
(The shoes are very dirty.)

Artículos definidos masculinos o femeninos—
Masculine or Feminine Definite Articles

There's more. In Spanish the definite article has four forms, depending on whether the noun is singular or plural, or *masculine* or *feminine*.

So articles are either "boys" or "girls," just like the nouns, and they match up with the nouns they are working with. It's pretty simple.

The "girl" definite articles end in *a*. But you probably already knew that.

Decimos:
　　La mesa
　　Las mesas

It's "muy fácil" (very easy) to figure out which article to use!

　　　　63　　　　Spanish Level 2—RBP0156

¿Qué palabra es la correcta?—Which word is correct?

Follow the example and circle the correct definite article according to whether the noun is singular or plural, masculine or feminine.

1. A papá le gusta ((la) el los las) salsa fresca.
   (Dad likes the salsa fresca.)

2. (La El Los Las) gatos prefieren el pescado.
   (The cats prefer fish.)

3. ¿Dónde está (la el los las) pelota de futból?
   (Where is the soccer ball?)

4. (La El Los Las) amigos miran las tarjetas de beisból todos los días.
   (The friends look at baseball cards every day.)

5. (La El Los Las) bebé está llorando por mamá.
   (The baby is crying for Mom.)

6. Rosa lleva (la el los las) camiseta azul.
   (Rosa wears the blue T-shirt.)

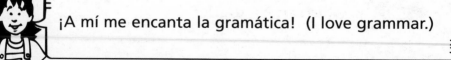

¡A mí me encanta la gramática! (I love grammar.)

¿Qué palabra es la correcta?—Which word is correct?

Circle the correct definite article according to whether the noun is singular or plural, masculine or feminine.

7. (La El Los Las) colas de los perros son largas.
(The tails of the dogs are long.)

8. Beto tiene (la el los las) gorra ahora.
(Beto has the ball cap now.)

9. Papá busca (la el los las) martillo.
(Dad looks for the hammer.)

10. Mamá pone (la el los las) cucharas en el lavaplatos.
(Mom puts the spoons in the dishwasher.)

11. Rosa juega con (la el los las) gato.
(Rosa plays with the cat.)

12. Beto ayuda a lavar (la el los las) perro.
(Beto helps to wash the dog.)

¡Yo no! (Not me!)

Artículos definidos plurales—Plural Articles

Write the correct article—*el, la, los,* or *las*—in front of the nouns below.

1. Beto prefiere __**la**__ silla grande.
(Beto prefers the big chair.)

2. Rosa prefiere _____ piso cuando está mirando
televisión.
(Rosa prefers the floor when she's watching
television.)

3. Mamá lee _____ libros.
(Mom reads the books.)

4. El bebé trata de comerse _____ comida del perro.
(The baby tries to eat the dog's food.)

5. Papá habla por _____ teléfono
(Dad talks on the telephone.)

¡Bien!
(Good!)

Artículos definidos plurales—Plural Articles

Write the correct article—*el, la, las,* or *los*—in front of the nouns below.

6. _____ niños se comen todas _____ galletas.
(The children eat all of the cookies.)

7. Mamá visita a _____ vecinos.
(Mom visits with the neighbors.)

8. _____ gatos duermen casi todo el día.
(The cats sleep almost the whole day.)

9. _____ familia Valenzuela habla español con nosotros.
(The Valenzuela family speaks Spanish with us.)

10. ¿Está limpia _____ ropa de los niños?
(Is the children's clothing clean?)

¿Dónde?—Where do the following items belong?

Fill in the blanks with the correct Spanish words that match the pictures.

cepillo

Word Bank

inodoro	loción	bañera	cepillo
cama	ropero	camiseta	zapatos

¿Dónde?—Where do the following items belong?

Fill in the blanks with the correct Spanish words that match the pictures.

Word Bank

martillo	cinta métrica	sierra	cerca
paseo	césped	árbol	alicates

¿Qué cuarto?—Which Room?

Write the correct name for the room in the space provided.

bathroom	kitchen
living room	study
basement	garage
bedroom	nursery

Word Bank

garaje	dormitorio
sala	estudio
cocina	el cuarto del bebé
baño	sótano

Artículos indefinidos—
Indefinite articles

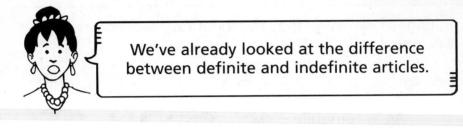

We've already looked at the difference between definite and indefinite articles.

Indefinite articles are not specific.

Let's review the difference:

Pick <u>a</u> book to read.
Pick <u>the</u> book about baseball.

The indefinite article here is <u>a</u> because we are talking about any book.

In English the indefinite article are the words "a," "an," or "some."

Artículos indefinidos plurales—
Plural Indefinite Articles

In English we know that the indefinite articles are *a*, *an*, or *some*.

We say:
A hammer
An automobile
Some tools

When you're talking about non-specific tools you'll use the indefinite.

In Spanish the indefinite article changes, depending on whether the noun is singular or plural.

Decimos:
<u>Un</u> martillo   (*A* hammer)
<u>Unos</u> martillos   (*Some* hammers)

Write the correct article, *un* or *unos* in front of the nouns below.

1. Leo _____ libro cada semana.
(I read a book every week.)

2. El bebé juega con _____ juguetes.
(The baby plays with some toys.)

3. _____ amigos nos visitan esta noche.
(Some friends are visiting us tonight.)

4. Mamá quiere _____ zapatos nuevos.
(Mom wants some new shoes.)

Artículos indefinidos masculinos o femininos—Masculine or Feminine Indefinite Articles

There's more. In Spanish the indefinite article, like the definite article, has four forms, depending on whether the noun is singular or plural, or masculine or feminine.

Indefinite articles are either "boys" or "girls" and they match up with the nouns they are working with.

You probably already guessed that the "girl' definite articles use the letter a.

Decimos:

<u>Una</u> camiseta	(*A* T-shirt)
<u>Unas</u> camisetas	(*Some* T-shirts)

It's "muy fácil" (very easy) to figure out which indefinite article to use!

¿Qué palabra es la correcta?—Which word is correct?

Circle the correct Indefinite Article according to whether it is singular or plural, masculine or feminine as shown.

1. Papá quiere ((un) una unas unos) carro nuevo.
(Dad wants a new car.)

2. (Un Una Unas Unos) personas cantan en español.
(Some people are singing in Spanish.)

3. ¿Quieres comerte (un una unas unos) burrito?
(Do you want to eat a burrito?)

4. Hay (un una unas unos) niña a la puerta.
(A girl is at the door.)

5. El perro se come (un una unas unos) juguete del bebé.
(The dog eats one of the baby's toys.)

6. Beto, busca (un una unas unos) camiseta limpia.
("Beto, look for a clean T-shirt.")

Tengo sed. Necesito un refresco.
(I'm thirsty. I need a soda.)

¿Qué palabra es la correcta?—Which word is correct?

Circle the correct Indefinite Article according to whether it is singular or plural, masculine or feminine as shown.

7. Hay (un una unas unos) martillos muy pesados.
(Some hammers are very heavy.)

8. Hay (un una unas unos) pelota en la entrada de coches.
(There's a ball in the driveway.)

9. Mamá mezcla (un una unas unos) bol de guacamole.
(Mom mixes a bowl of guacamole.)

10. Ellos pintan (un una unas unos) cuartos de la casa.
(They paint some rooms in the house.)

11. Papá toma (un una unas unos) taza de café cada mañana.
(Dad drinks a cup of coffee every morning.)

12. ¿Puedo invitar a (un una unas unos) amigo a jugar aquí hoy?
(May I have a friend to play here today?)

Página de respuestas—Answer Pages

Page 3
1. el hermano   2. el perro
3. el papá   4. el bebé
5. la hermana   6. la mamá
7. el gato

Page 10
tomate—tomato
semillas—seeds
cebolla—onion   ajo—garlic
jalapeño—jalapeño (chili pepper)
cucharada—tablespoon

Page 11
tortillas de maiz fritas—tortilla chips
cucharadita—teaspoon
sal—salt   bol—bowl
refrigerador—refrigerator
lima—lime

Page 12

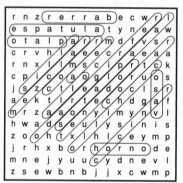

Page 16
cama—bed   tocador—dresser
ropero—clothes closet
cartel—poster
almohada—pillow
juguete—toy

Page 17
gorra—cap
chaqueta—jacket
falda—skirt
zapatos—shoes
pantalones—pants

Page 23

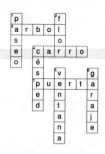

Page 27
These nouns should be circled:
cebolla, puerta, comida, ventana, cocina, gorra, familia

Page 28
inodoro—toilet
cepillo para el pelo—hairbrush
lavamanos—sink   peine—comb
toalla—towel
maquinilla de afeitar—safety razor

Page 29
creama de afeitar—shaving cream
jábon—soap
loción—lotion
bañera—bathtub
espejo—mirro
champú—shampoo

Page 33

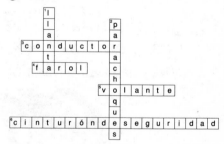

Page 38
These nouns should be circled:
dormitorio, libro, vaso, patio, sueño, cepillo, lavabo, zapato, cinco

Página de respuestas—Answer Pages

Page 39

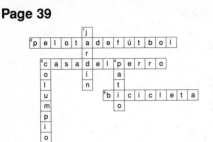

Page 40
From left to right, top to bottom:
oler, brincar, gritar, llorar

Page 44

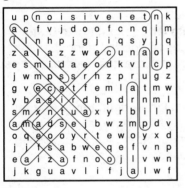

Page 45

silla—toilet

sofá—couch

alfombra—rug

cojín—cushion

estéreo—stereo

cortina—curtain

mesa—table

lámpara—lamp

cama—bed

televisión—television

pintura—painting

Page 47
hablo, hablas, habla, hablamos, hablan

canto, cantas, canta, cantamos, cantan

limpio, limpias, limpia, limpiamos, limpian

corto, cortas, corta, cortamos, cortan

descanso, descansas, descansa, descansamos, descansan

Page 48

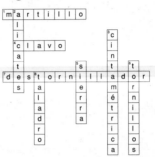

Page 49
barro, barres, barre, barremos, barren

corro, corres, corre, corremos, corren

bebo, bebes, bebe, bebemos, beben

dependo, dependes, depende dependemos, dependen

leo, lees, lee, leemos, leen

Page 50
vivo, vives, vive, vivimos, viven

subo, subes, sube, subimos, suben

escribo, escribes, escribe, escribimos, escriben

uno, unes, une, unimos, unen

cubro, cubres, cubre, cubrimos, cubren

Página de respuestas—Answer Pages

Page 52–53
1. hablan
2. llora
3. Comemos
4. corren
5. limpia
6. vive
7. beben
8. sube
9. canta
10. leemos
11. Barro
12. corta

Page 55

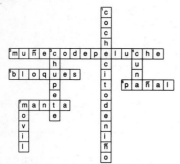

Page 58
gato—cat
hocico—muzzle
cola—tail
piel—fur
collar—collar
perro—dog

Page 60

w r x j c (o i r o t i r c s e)
g t t r l k k r s d e l j t e
(x) h x m q h e o b i b g l n s
a c i n u t b b j e a o k i s
(f (c o m p u t a d o r a) g f q
e o k y u t (i m p r e s o r a)
j z p i s (g r a p a d o r a) d
(t a r u s a b a l e d o b u c)
e h v n n v g r j i t w t j k
l b h q e (a i r e t n a t s e)
e y (l e p a p e d a m s e r) r
f v g t m q s d i l s n i w p
o j c x a x n b p y c z c d a
n z h v d a l o n p j x c y k
(o) q c g a l b y i z n l s x v

Page 62
1. el
2. los
3. el
4. Los

Page 64
1. la
2. Los
3. la
4. Los
5. El
6. la

Page 65
7. Las
8. la
9. el
10. las
11. el
12. el

Page 66
1. la
2. el
3. los
4. la
5. el

Page 67
6. Los, las
7. los
8. Los
9. La
10. la

Page 68
From left to right, top to bottom:
cepillo, loción, inodoro, bañera
cama, zapatos, ropero, camiseta

Page 69
From left to right, top to bottom:
martillo, sierra, alicates, cinta
métrica, árbol, cerca, césped,
paseo

Page 70
From left to right, top to bottom:
baño, cocina, sala, estudio,
sótano, garaje, dormitorio,
el cuarto del bebé

Page 72
1. un
2. unos
3. unos
4. unos

Page 74–75
1. un
2. Unas
3. un
4. una
5. un
6. una
7. unos
8. una
9. un
10. unos
11. una
12. un